Pandemic Poems

Pandemic Poems

First Wave

Olive Senior

© 2021 by Olive Senior

All rights reserved. No part of this publication may be reproduced, stored in a retrieval system or transmitted in any form or by any means – electronic, mechanical, photocopying, and recording or otherwise – without prior written permission from the author. The exception would be brief passages by a reviewer in a newspaper or magazine or online. To perform any of the above is an infringement of copyright law.

ISBN 978-1-7774523-0-8 (print)
ISBN 978-1-7774523-2-2 (Kindle)
ISBN 978-1-7774523-1-5 (ePub)

Cover illustration: Fridtjof Nansen (1861–1930), https://en.wikipedia.org/wiki/Fridtjof_Nansen), Aurora Borealis drawing, University of Illinois Archives Exhibits. https://archives.library.illinois.edu/exhibits/items/show/40.

Cover design by Robert Harris
Book design by Sharmila Mohammed

Published 2021 by Olive Senior, Toronto, Canada
www.olivesenior.com

CONTENTS

Preface	vii
Concordance	xi
The Poems	1
Acknowledgements	93

PREFACE

These poems appear in the order in which they were written and posted on my Twitter and Facebook pages between May and September – the Covid-19 summer of 2020. An alphabetical listing is also provided because it was the pandemic lexicon – new words and phrases or old words repurposed – that first got me engaged.

Each poem is a riff on a word or phrase trending at the period. Presenting them in sequence offers a timeline of the way events unfolded and how the language and preoccupations kept changing in response. By the time I came to the end, I could see where our vocabulary had solidified with few new words entering the glossary and the same ones presenting with careworn familiarity.

The pandemic has brought about not just challenges to health but deeper challenges to transforming society and culture. Where 'flattening the curve', 'sanitize' or 'keep your distance' once commanded our attention, the death of George Floyd and the subsequent need to affirm Black Lives Matter erupted into and shifted the international discourse and the vocabulary. And while the end of summer has been dominated by 'reopening', 'rise in cases' and 'vaccine', another shadow is inescapably looming: climate change and the many manifestations of sickness of the Earth itself.

I have not stopped writing Pandemic Poems, but the end of summer seemed a good time to pause.

The poems are presented here as they were written, with a few very minor changes to language or punctuation which do not alter them in any substantive way. I regard these poems as more of a sharing with a community than a purely literary endeavour; what I needed to say was often more important than the saying of it (which is not how I usually write). I am interested in memorializing the historic moment we are living through, with capturing the zeitgeist, literally 'the spirit of the time'.

A few of these poems utilize the words of others – a legitimate poetic form known as 'found poetry', which employs scraps of material from various sources – newspapers, advertisements, tweets, headlines and the like. When the entire poem consists of found material, as in 'Poetic Eavesdropping', it is called a cento (meaning patchwork), a form that goes back to at least the second century.

I used these 'found' words where I felt they would be most powerful, presenting the authentic voices of those actually feeling it and knowing it, such as ICU workers, essential workers, people experiencing a Covid-19 death of a loved one and unable to mourn, as well as witty commentators on topical news events. Where exact words of others are used, I have put them within quotation marks or in italics.

I started writing these poems as a way of keeping myself engaged and not falling into depression, but I soon realized I was inside a loop that bound me to readers, many of whom told me they waited for a poem each day as it helped to articulate what they were going through.

We are in a truly historic moment: everyone across the globe sharing the same experience and – for the first time – having the technology available to transmit our response in real time. We are using words that everyone in the world is using at the same time, in their own languages: this is an extraordinary happenstance. More than anything else, these poems capture the paradox that even as we are forced into consciousness of being a part of the world, we are at the same time forced to be apart.

I like to think that the instant call-and-response offered by poetry in the moment takes us back to the dawn of humanity, where the tribe in a firelit circle gathered to listen – and react – to songs and stories of that day's events imparted by singer or bard or medicine man/woman, hunter or matriarch. And right down to our time, no song or story can be complete – can even have a beginning – without a listener or a reader.

To all of my readers I can only say, thank you for becoming a part of the circle, for nourishing with your responses.

I offer these Pandemic Poems as a small contribution to work that artists all over the world are making to signal – in the words of the poet Stevie Smith – that we are 'waving, not drowning'.

CONCORDANCE

A   Adjustment / 23

B   Bees / 82
    Bird 1-0 Technology / 75
    Bread / 67
    Breathe / 36

C   Cherry Blossoms / 9
    Chillin . . . / 69
    Circle / 83
    Coloured / 55
    Concert / 58
    Contact Tracing / 31
    Corona / 18
    Cranes / 17
    Cruise / 73

D   Disposable / 71
    Domestic Violence / 12

E   Ease / 84
    Empty / 77

F	Facing It / 38
	Fight / 13
	Flag / 32
	Flattening the Curve / 1
G	Gamble / 81
	Goodbye (that's no way to say...) / 20
	Green News / 54
H	Hair / 48
	Hand / 10
	Hero / 46
	Hope / 70
I	ICU / 24
	Injection / 19
	Invasive Species / 43
	Invisible / 60
J	Just / 68
K	Knee / 45
L	Less / 85
	Landfall / 89
	Liberty / 91
	Locked Out / 8
M	Mask / 4
	Misplaced / 59
N	Necessity / 34
	Negotiate / 87
	Normal / 47
	Numbers / 65
O	One / 30

P	Pause / 40
	Poetic Eavesdropping / 64
Q	Quarantine Roots / 7
R	Racist Robots / 63
	Riddle / 42
S	Separation / 27
	Simple / 39
	Smile / 51
	Social Distancing / 3
	Socially Distanced Events / 53
	Sweep / 72
T	Time Wasting / 57
	Touch / 15
U	Underlying Conditions / 16
	Unwanted Guests / 28
V	Vaccine / 44
W	Waiting / 5
	Warning / 79
	Wave, Second / 61
	Wildlife / 22
	Workers / 41
	Wrong-Sided / 76
X	X-road / 25
Y	Youth / 50
Z	Zoom / 33

F for Flattening (the curve)

We have beaten nature down
Exalted straightness.

But somewhere, are things we can never control:
Wildness always trying to break in.

When and where, unnoticed for how long
did this bump in the road emerge
this curve
that so urgently
needs flattening now?

IV.—Development of Wireless Telegraphy. Scene in Hyde Park.
[These two figures are not communicating with one another. The lady is receiving an amatory message and the gentleman some racing results.]

S for Social Distancing

What if you

wanted to

keep me

at arm's length

anyway?

M for Mask

Masqueraders know the protective power of masks assumed in Carnivals each year to placate the spirit Death, embody the supernatural.

Now, Death is here. Masks for everyone is streetwear.

Except in this theatre. No wild carnivalesque disorder. No summoning the supernatural. Here mask-wearers offer silent intercessions in communal rooms, wrestle Death for Life in choreographed routines: calm, concentration, skill, compassion, order.

Only when the masks are off do they reveal the traces: the daily struggle with Death imprinted on their faces.

W for Waiting

On March 22, the government pulled the Covid-19 emergency cord in India: 13,500 daily passenger trains a day and 25 million passengers came to a full stop.

At Varanasi Junction, an ancient city on the Ganges, some got off but never got on another train again; departure signboards blank as total lockdown began.

Fifty disparate souls en route to far-flung destinations are still stuck there, confined to the waiting room, forbidden to leave the station, desperate.

Is this life? asks Laxmi, 700 miles from home and children.

From destinations even further: parents with children, construction worker, manager, pilgrims, students, lawyer and a marketing pro

Waiting.

Enter Anand Mohan the station manager who organizes them. Child's play when the station is used to handling 100,000 passengers a day. Washrooms, medical checks, three meals a day, hot tea and yoga classes thrown in.

He tells them to avoid the news. Too depressing. For uplift he arranges daily showings of the multi-part serial

Hindu epics: the *Ramayana* and the *Mahabharata*,
which demonstrate, Mohan says, *Evil dies . . . good
prevails . . . if you do the right thing.*

His charges sleep on benches, thin rugs on the floor.
In the cavernous waiting room they bond . . . *complete
strangers . . . we talk. We share our pain.*

Three weeks on; departure boards stay blank.
No one knows when passenger trains will roll again.
The nationwide lockdown has been extended.

* * *

We, far away, can read Varanasi Junction as a play, a
novel, a film we've already seen.

Or simply as a metaphor for all of us who are now

(Is this life?)

Locked in and

Waiting.

The original story appeared in the *Washington Post*, 15 April 2020,
reporters Joanna Slater and Tana Dutta.

Q for Quarantine Roots

Did you see that report from Lansing, Michigan,
where the good citizens rode into town demanding
an end to lockdown? ('A pearl-clutching moment
of the Trumpanzees,' a critic murmured.)

You can't even get paint or fertilizer, an angry veteran
     complained
while an older woman in a car to the cameras
     bared her grey head, deploring her inability
     to secure a hairdo or hair dye.

That's a hair-don't, jibed the Twittersphere.
Dyeing to die. Who's gonna see you when the casket's closed?

And a double whammy:
*At the cemetery they will take care of all your gardening
     needs;
at the mortuary they will take care of your roots . . .*

I'm trying not to laugh as I hide my uncombed grey locks
'Quarantine roots' being a deadly serious offence these
     days.

   HEADLINE APRIL 11: Walmart CEO says we are in the 'hair
     colour' phase of panic buying.

L for Locked Out

Some things are beyond the cutting edge of poems.
Like this true story (BBC report, with photographs)
of this widow in a far-off land, in lockdown: no income,
six children and no food. She puts water in the cooking pot,
adds stones and tells them to wait for soup. They know
she is lying; their crying alerts a neighbour who arranges
assistance. Thus that old Stone Soup tale is re-enacted.

But this is not meant to be an allegory of craftiness
or kindness.
You can read it simply as a reflection
on how an invisible virus can make visible
that other pandemic: the collateral damage
to half the world without the means to withstand it.

C for Cherry Blossoms

Sickness blooms. Parks and gardens are closed to us.
This year, we cannot witness
the splendour of the blossoming cherry trees.

What is sad is that the cherry trees couldn't care less.
Without us, they will still bloom and show off
their splendiferous dress.

H for Hand

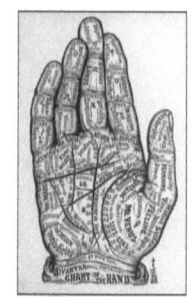

Days when a handshake was as good as a signature or your word. And handsome was a compliment. Handy meant 'really good at' everything or being one's right hand.

Days of our youth when a hand-delivered letter was often signed S.W.A.K. But kisses are banned now, love-tokens proffered at arms-length, out of reach or second-hand.

My Grannie's 'Hand Wash Hand' mantra no longer means reciprocity but: Look to Your Own. Wash Hands Frequently. Stay Home or Stay 18 Hands Apart (4 inches the length of a hand).

Each day we glad-hand our 'heroes': our hospital and health workers who uphold Hand as symbol of Fortitude and Fidelity while they handcuff Death or try to keep it a hand's breadth from our door.

Our leaders caution: All hands on deck now until we get a handle on it and can pull together to a brighter shore where we will unhand each other, disband to return to a (new) normal world.

*

Not quite so fast, my friends. The crisis is out of our hands but not entirely. See the handwriting on the wall: WHAT WILL WE HAND DOWN TO POSTERITY?

No longer can we wash our hands of what offends us – those living hand-to-mouth. We cannot say in the face of distress: our hands are full; our hands are tied; our hands are clean.

A handout is not a handsome gift. What would be handier is learning how to slice the pie and pass it hand to hand so everyone can take an equal share.

D for Domestic Violence

As if the sickness outside
has entered here: the fear,
the choking, the gasping
for breath. But no, that one
is silent and invisible, named,
with an exit strategy.

For this one
the 'shadow pandemic'
there is only
the uncertainty,
the battering,
the shivering,
the fear,
the choking,
the gasping
for breath.

And
this
blocked exit.

F for Fight

Some are fighting mad at the language of leaders
describing the Covid-19 battle: 'Boris is fighting
the infection.'

'It implies that those who lost the fight
didn't fight hard enough,' says one objecting to
applying 'fight' to illness.

Another embraces the language as affirmation:
'Cancer fights dirty.'

And then there is the voice of reason: *The patient
is not fighting the disease; the disease
leaves the patient fighting to function.*

As the body gears for fight or flight
Fighting words can wound or uplift.

T for Touch

Though 'skin hunger' is real, we are told,
the need for touch biological,
hard-wired in us, how long after
we leave lockdown will the fear
of contagion keep us starving ourselves
of touch?

U for Underlying Conditions

A pandemic is a democratic event, we are told,
the great equalizer: which makes us all equally at risk.
But the toll keeper knows who goes first – the aged
and sickly, the immunocompromised and those
on the darker side who are being taken
disproportionately quickly.

It is not the melanin, no, Death has no prejudice.
But it can unmask society's pathology, laying bare
the sickness that was always there: the social and
economic inequalities that provide Death
with one's address.

Studies show: *Disempowerment makes people ill.*

Factories might be closed, but the manufacture
of inequality never ceases. Communities of colour
are the most exposed. As the pressure of
underlying conditions increases, they are the ones
most quickly summoned to pay the toll.

C for Cranes

All over our city, mechanical cranes sit still
like stiff-necked angry birds; construction halted
in mid-flight.

Meanwhile, live cranes, unstoppable, announce
Spring's coming, millions in migratory flights
cross distances to mating dances.

I hope those cranes don't fly over our city where
our cranes, still and stiff-necked, on seeing them,
would grind their mechanical teeth, weep, and topple.

C for Corona

Corona from the Greek meaning 'anything curved'
    elevated long ago to mean a circle of light around
    a luminous body, like the moon; a halo for the
    solar deity

from there to symbolic associations of the circle with
    perfection: the ring-shaped crown for both royals
    and the divine

then sliding a little lower as the seal of victory or
    achievement: the laurel wreath, the leafy crown,
    for heroes, generals, or sporting stars

to floral garlands for beauty and pleasure at transitional
    times: wreaths for May queens or June brides.

How then   this   collapse   of   the   halo,
    the crown, on to
    the heads of incompetent
    but powerful clowns whose lasting achievement
    will be presiding over   the distribution
        of funeral wreaths   in the service of a
            greater dictator
                named Corona.

I for Injection

Someone had to inject some sense into this:

The manufacturer:
Under no circumstance should our disinfectant products be administered into the human body.

The UK government's medical advisor:
... nobody should be injecting anything.

A doctor on Twitter:
OFFS *don't do this. I don't need the extra work.*

G for Goodbye
(that's no way to say...)

Yes, this is the new way.

Bodies piled up in makeshift morgues in nursing homes
Bodies of those who died alone discovered long after
Bodies in communal burial grounds.
Bodies left...

If so fortunate, goodbye to loved ones in an ICU through a video call by caring medical staff: *It was among the heaviest moments I've encountered in my short clinical career.*
. . . .
Couldn't visit him in hospital.
Couldn't say goodbye.
Couldn't have a funeral.
Can't have a Shiva house.
. . . .
Even if a funeral is allowed, there's social distancing. *How are you supposed to grieve when you can't touch?*
. . . .

How many years later will this pandemic hit?

While waiting for the traffic light to change.
While brushing your teeth one morning.
In the middle of making love.
Punching down the dough.
Laughing.

The choking need to say goodbye.

The grieving.

W for Wildlife

While the human animals are penned up inside
those other animals come out to gaze:
explorers in a new-found land.

Mountain goats, lambs, flamingos, sea lion, sheep,
racoon, jackals, foxes, fallow deer, wild boars,
wandering about in territory once considered exclusively
'ours'.

This so-called invasion is not an invasion at all, say the experts: *Our cities are part of nature. Animals normally live in those parts we don't use; are an unseen presence, like ghosts.*

Animals in zoos and wildlife parks in lockdown are so lonely for human visitors, some have also gone looking. Rhinos and giraffes turn up for their scheduled 'meet the people' appearances. Monkeys in Thailand missing snacks from tourists 'brawl over a cup of yoghurt'. Sika deer in Japan without rice-cracker treats wander into town to nibble anything. And an aquarium pleads for the public to video-chat its eels because human contact is missing.

When humans are turned loose in cities once again, what will happen to these 'ghosts'? To the wild?

A for Adjustment

Refugees do it every day
Slip into the unknown
alone, maybe,
withstand what we will never know
heading for the Promised Land.

And we who live in the Promised Land
now have a taste of it.
Not of what they have endured, no way.
Just a twinge of
that gut-wrenching
seismic shift.

I for ICU

POEMS FOUND ON THE ICU FLOOR

During a 12-hour shift
I take a single break.
Our patients are so sick
we don't want to leave them.

So many sedated patients on ventilators
they all look the same. Like something
out of a horror movie.
As if we are just waiting for them to wake up.
. . . .
He was one of ours.
A health care worker.
We were with him.
We prayed.
We held his hand.
His family couldn't be there.
. . . .
We connect family and patient
by videoconference or phone
even when patients can no longer speak.
The loved ones call out:

Daddy, wake up. Come home.

X for X-road

In my dictionary X is the least of letters
often a symbol or modifier –
an X-rated film, a kiss, an examination error.

Married to *e* on the page it seems formidable:
E(xcise)
E(xpunge)
E(xecute)
E(xclude)
E(xtinction)
E(xtubate)
E(xtremity)
E(xit)

Once it casts off the *e*, X goes its own way
heads for the highway, stops at the X-road
place of power, possibilities and choice
the place we are standing now, directionless

waiting for X to mark the spot

the right path
to (E)x

S for Separation

Six feet: two metres apart
is where we need to stand now
to 'social distance'
to avert disaster
trying not to think that
if this distance fails, we fall
to lie six feet under.

U for Unwanted Guests

It's like that horror movie where you can no longer resist the pounding at your door. You are forced to let them in, the unwanted visitor, the one you expect to never see again, hoping this will be a short-term stay.

One day, if you survive, they will leave you masked and shaken, broke and reeling, but alive.

You know in your heart the danger might return though you double-lock your door, you isolate, you sanitize. Until you find the nerve to step outside while social distancing. You breathe in, surprised to find the slowed-down world exhaling a cleaner air. You take heart from the positive new vibrations: Reopening. Retail Rebound. Rebooting. Until you read this headline:

COVID-19 MIGHT NEVER GO AWAY – W.H.O.

Well, I don't know. Don't we survive those other unwanted guests that are always turning up – like influenza and the common cold?

*

Besides, we have a more pressing pandemic to worry about, one that is very old but has speeded up from Covid-19 effects:

MALNUTRITION IS NOW THE LEADING CAUSE OF ILL HEALTH AND DEATH GLOBALLY (Global Nutrition Report 2020)

And do you think this one will never turn up at your door?

O for One

As one alone, I sometimes wish I were with another
or two or three in lockdown together.
But then again, I think maybe the two or three
in lockdown together by now are wishing
they were one, alone.

C for Contact Tracing

When I see 'contact tracing' it makes me want to write a letter to someone I lost long ago, who left no forwarding address, vanished without a trace. Feel sorry now that I did not hire a private detective or some such cliché.

But nostalgia counts for nothing when everything is driven by exigence: contact tracing a kind of policing to tag everyone who had contact with someone testing positive in the hope of stopping a viral spread.

Contact can never be considered again as simply touch and go. Someone will find out you were close once. Yes, the whole world is communicable. And yet with 71 million displaced, so many can still vanish without a trace.

F for Flag

'Showing the flag' in some countries has taken on a desperate new meaning. No longer asserting a claim to territory or a symbol of victory, flag waving is now the signal of surrender to hunger and need; an iconography of individual misery.

Those desperate for help line major streets and highways waving squares of cloth, sometimes colour coded: white rags for hunger; red the need for medicine, black, yellow or blue to signal woman, child or older person in danger of violence.

The poor have become the standard bearers of a new reality: lockdown only works for those with the means to sustain it. Those locked out of society have found a way to signal that they are flagging; the body itself at half-mast.

Z for Zoom . . .

. . . which makes us think of the superhero zooming in from outer space to save Gotham City or Planet Earth.

So now we are Zooming all together in the teleconferencing village: working, learning, partying from home. Leading to Zoom bombings by uninvited guests, Zoom weddings, Zoom babysitters, Zoom-almost-sex (*It. . . feels as though heat is being exchanged between our screens . . .*) and then Zumping or Zoom breakups. As one who had dumped his previous girlfriend by text-message could attest: *Doing it by Zoom is a bit more honest as you're saying it in real time and seeing the whites of their eyes and the tears.*

Those who are Zoomed out or suffering from Zoom fatigue might well ask, 'How can I get out of this?' Rescue might come from something as wildly improbable as a comic book hero zooming in to save us. But already there is an element celestial: you can sit for a while in a waiting room while a Zoom master decides to let you in; just like St Peter at the Pearly Gates.

N for Necessity

Exempting the Easter Bunny, the Tooth Fairy, and Santa Claus from lockdown shouldn't give us pause.

But look at what some leaders considered necessary for their citizens:

In Paris: wine, food and chocolate sales, exempted,
　as expected.

In some US states: gun stores and marijuana dispensaries.

In Australia: off-licence liquor stores and toy shops (with a run on jigsaw puzzles).

India's national lockdown exempted the IT sector and Bangladeshi garment factories reopened under
　Western pressure.

Ontario exempted liquor stores with the argument that closure would have widespread deleterious effect on mental health.

South Africa didn't get that message and banned the sale of alcohol, cigarettes and takeout food, leading to the expected liquor store break-ins and drone deliveries. That country then saw a massive increase in the sale of pineapples. Pineapples became the main ingredient in homemade wine.

Necessity Knows No Law.

B for Breathe

It takes one's breath away: a man dying during a pandemic that takes away one's breath, no ventilator but one brave spectator, recording

his last breath, his need *please*

somebody

taking the knee on the neck from men who from birth breathed in tainted air, imbibed a foul history, burning crosses

still smouldering

i can't breathe

like the hot breath of anger consuming the cities
we have breathed this before
this white heat this
burning sensation in the throats of
the numerous ones held down and

mama
mama
i cant

Come on, George Floyd, breathe in the timeless rhythm of Mother Earth waiting for you, for all her lost children, for justice

I'm through
I'm through

F for Facing It

Let us face it. The home screen invites a different gaze. *Headshots are the new hemlines*, as a *Guardian* reporter expressed it; the home space and the contents of background bookshelves now avidly deconstructed.

This is about learning to read again: the naked face indoors, the masked face without. The one revealing too much, the other leaving us perpetually searching for cues.

S for Simple

Tuning out . . .
greeted by dive-bombing Red-winged Blackbird on nest
   duty
guarding this little bit of wild in the heart of the city.
Ducks in the pond. Turtles on a rock. Woods
resounding with bird song.
Life suddenly reduced to simple.
Our world of sorrow has forced us to close our door
but there is this other world out there
forever open
carrying on
as before.

P for Pause

Twenty-two seconds of silence on the air. The time
it took for the prime minister of Canada to marshal
a response to a reporter asking for his opinion on
President Trump's actions on the George Floyd affair.
Such a crime! The pause, that is. In broadcasting: dead air.

But this is not about politicians and diplomacy. Let us
focus only on that interval between thought and speech.
Let us wish there was more of this, not just on the air but
everywhere.

Since our own lives are on pause anyway,
this might be a good time to practise hesitation.
Pause between speech and action, between impulse and
activity. Take as long as you need. There is no timekeeper
monitoring the length of your pause, the only marker,
perhaps, would be the slowing down of your heartbeat.

W for Workers

Once we were faceless. Then service workers.
Now labelled Essential, we have become 'Heroes'.
Do not call us heroes. That's the kind of rhetoric
that sends young people off to war though we too
are in this struggle because we have no choice.
We are on the frontlines yes but stop trying to speak
for us. We have a voice. We are risk-takers.
But we don't want praise. We just want a decent wage.

Calling me a hero only makes you feel better.
We are not heroes. We are hostages. Work or starve.

I feel like essential just stands for exhausted and expendable.
(Grocery worker)

I'm essential and I get a starvation wage for others to eat.
(Fast-food worker)

All day, using hand sanitizer between every customer,
my hands have become raw. My muscles ache from all the
extra wiping down of our conveyer belt.
(Grocery store cashier)

The distance principle, six feet between people, does not
work in agriculture.
(Strawberry picker)

I'm not a hero. I'm just in debt.

R for Riddle

It cannot be seen but it permeates our lives
It cannot walk but we enable it to travel
It has no body but it captures our breath
It has no teeth but it conquers flesh
It plants nothing but it harvests souls
It has no authority but it forces isolation
It has no voice but it commands every nation

What is it?

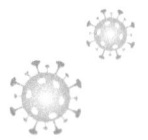

I for Invasive Species

Soon there will be guide books on how to safely navigate the perils of the outdoors: jogging on suburban or city streets, walking in a public park, peacefully demonstrating, birding while Black. If you are a certain pigmentation you cannot simply sit around on your doorstep killing time: you might invite arrest or attack.

But shouldn't there be manuals for spaces that are considered safe, such as inside your own home? There, you can still fall prey to invasive species called domestic violence. Or mistaken identity. Or accidental homicide.

V for Vaccine

How quickly Covid-19 has been upstaged
by a more insidious injection of hate into
the Black body that has gone viral.
Boots on the ground
and no social etiquette required.
Unless there is rigorous commitment
to eradicating poisonous infection,
no vaccine to counteract this one
will ever be found.

K for Knee

Knee has become an expression of articulation
in more ways than one.
To affirm that Black Lives Matter
a lot of genuflection has been going on.
How much of this is a knee-jerk reflex action
to ride the populist bandwagon?
Or is this truly a moment for all of us
from bended knee
to rise and pivot
to aim for that goal
that will finally secure
what we stand for.

H for Hero

We keep trying to reframe 'hero' in the refracted light
of those we have been told to call heroes all our lives.
In the current pandemic, we are embracing as heroes
those of a different demographic.

But while we are clapping our hands and banging pans
every night to cheer them on, they are tired of it.
Don't call us heroes, they remonstrate. Best to ignore that.
Even the experts are stumped: 'Hero Studies'
is a newly created psychological field.

Perhaps we need to toss out those imprinted images
and biographies and statues and history books
and just confess: A hero is simply an exceptional person
who will put themselves at great personal risk
to do what needs to be done, regardless.

N for Normal

Please don't speak of the 'new normal'. Those two words are not a pair. New refers to something fresh and unused, not second hand. Normal implies the usual: the regular, typical, conformity with a standard (the word after all comes from *norma*, the carpenter's rule or square).

OK. There are things in our old life that we all want to return to. But there is also a lot we need to jettison. Think of it as moving to a new house to start afresh. We pack everything useful and treasured to take with us but we also leave behind a lot of rubbish.

There is no going back for any of us. The old house is on fire. A Band-Aid labelled 'Normal' will not smother it. Time perhaps to get out the old carpenter's square and recalibrate it.

H for Hair

Is self-care our measure of normal life? Consider this: When Italy reopened, there was more demand for beauty salons than restaurants and shops.

We know of the hemline factor mirroring the rise and fall of the economy. And then there is the Lipstick Index, the turning to less expensive indulgencies in hard times – women (apparently) will always purchase a small beauty item to get a fix. Now with mask wearing and eye makeup it's the Mascara Index trending.

But hair continues to be the greatest preoccupation for both men and women. Advice proliferates: Self-colour or let it go? Shave it or save it? Black hair? That requires an entire poem.

'Haircut' is the most googled beauty treatment in lockdown with many professionals of course advising against it. But: *This is a pandemic. I might die. Why not cut my hair?* Others airily advise: *Add a life skill. Cut your own hair.* So I did.

British Columbia's health minister ruefully cautioned (after cutting hers): *They say the number one thing not to do in a pandemic is cut your own hair.* Clearly, her prime minister is listening. Canadians with nothing better to do are measuring time passing by the growing length of their leader's hair when they see him daily on the air.

Y for Youth

The gap between young and old is widening.
Old people are living longer, and – some youth
complain – sucking up too much air. Don't worry,
coronavirus
is now taking care
of that.

They say
the aged are the carriers of a dying culture
the young the bearers of a new world order.

The wheels just
keep turning.

Every revolution
has its roots in history.

Youth and age might not always agree

but there is no fruit without a tree.

S for Smile

How do you signal smiling behind the mask?
How do you, in passing, convey friendliness?
The eyes have it, yes,
but what if they are behind glasses
or you are moving too fast to impress?
I know there are women out there
for whom face covering is normal
so you must have evolved ways
of communicating. Can you share
any secrets with us? This is also
making me think of face covering
getting in the way of people who
have difficulty hearing.
I hope no one is offended by
these questions. I'm simply perplexed.
If you are annoyed, don't revile me.
From behind the mask
simply throw me a smile.
I might get it.

S for Socially Distanced Events

I read with sadness that this year the Queen's Birthday
celebration was a 'socially distanced event' at Windsor
   Castle.
I feel for her as I have been to many such events myself,
though of course being the queen she would always be
the centre and never like me, really socially distanced.

And now the premier of the province in which I live
wants to ease lockdown restrictions by allowing 'social
   circles',
gatherings of 10 people or less who – I suppose in real life
– are not socially distanced. This is really catching on.
I have seen proposals for 'social bubbles' and for 'pods'.
I don't know what to make of this.

The last 'pod' I saw was in an aerial photograph of
15 cruise ships anchored near a deserted Caribbean islet,
looking indeed like a pod of idle whales which the pandemic
had left bereft. I wonder how soon these ships
will break out of that exile and resume their duty:
as conveyers of birthday celebrants, social circles
and the upwardly idle.

G for Green News

Somewhere, for a brief time
in this collective pause,
we are witnessing bluer skies,
purer water, cleaner air
and a friendlier world for bees.
A turning back to roots
with window gardening,
backyard planting
and soaring sales of seeds.

Know that every cutting
you put into the ground,
every seed you dig in,
feels like a little tickle
on the skin of Mother Earth
leaving her smiling
and wanting more.

C for Coloured

In case you hadn't noticed
the whole world is coloured.
Everything that lives
is saturated except those
who are off colour.

Now there are signs everywhere
saying Opening Soon.
The colours are preening themselves
and the birds will decide
who they want to sing for.

T for Time Wasting

OPENING TIME

Waste time	Spend time	Save time
While away time	Devote time to	Seize time
Pass time	Ahead of time	Make time
Mark time	In good time	Keep time
At whatever time	In no time	Measure time
Lose time	On time	Timetable

Endless time	For a time	Time sensitive
All the time	Another time	Time of one's life
Over time	In time	Time honoured
At one time	The nick of time	Time consuming
At the same time	Just in time	Time worn
Timeless	At that time	Time expired
Lifetime	Time out	

CLOSING TIME

C for Concert

This is not something I can keep mum about.

The Barcelona Liceu Opera House will reopen
on Monday with a string quartet playing Puccini's
Chrysanthemums to a packed audience
consisting of 2,292 potted plants.

The artistic director said he felt it appropriate to stage
this concert for the Biocene, with nature filling spaces
left empty by isolating humans. To whom the concert
will be livestreamed.

Although the plants might find the concert hall a bit
small after the great outdoors, I'm sure they will conduct
themselves with decorum; just the discreet nod, wave,
or palms put together, like any audience.

Nature is used to moving to its own rhythm anyway
and flowers are probably bored with serenades
from bumblebees and other suitors. They should find this
a welcome diversion.

It might start a trend. Soon, plants will be ordering up
their own jazz band from New Orleans, or reggae
recordings, or rappelling the four best soloists
from the Heavenly Choir.

M for Misplaced

'You don't belong here' is trending:
ownership of space based exclusively
on race. Doors once firmly locked
are bursting open everywhere.
Not in welcome. To enable
a spilling out of venom
directed at people walking, jogging,
birdwatching, sitting or simply
minding their own business
in the open air.

Ladies and gentlemen,
you'd go back inside if you understood
how misplaced is your claim;
ownership of space
is based on an entirely false premise.

On Mother Earth
we are all tenants,
the only difference
is the length assigned
each one of us
for our lease.

I for Invisible

How will we ever let go of the fear that each of us
could be carrying an invisible passenger, a viral ghost
that gives no sign, no demented banshee wailing,
until it takes away our breath?

Charms and spells against plague
have left us bare-faced and empty-handed.

With our puny mantras
do we stand the ghost of a chance
to outwit this other?

WASH HANDS

KEEP YOUR DISTANCE

COVER YOUR FACE

W for Wave, Second

Let's hope it will signal
waving, not drowning.

At School

R for Racist Robots

No. I. Am. Not. Making. This. Up.
Algorithms used by US courts for risk assessment
to reoffend are found to have a racial bias.
Just one example of how Artificial Intelligence
is already infected with the virus of inequality.
AI learns to predict by studying previous reports
to find patterns – information
that is already infused with human prejudices.
Garbage in. Garbage out.
To enter that Brave New World of AI,
we first need to deprogram humankind.
The future is tied to the past. AI, after all, is us.

P for Poetic Eavesdropping

'... *the coughing stopped, and we all hung, waiting, to hear what would come next.*'

'... *as well as a spike in birth rates later this year, one suspects divorce rates may also rise.*'

'*Where is everyone?*'

'Everybody is either panic buying or panic disinfecting, or panic something . . .'

'How are we ending phone conversations now that we don't have anywhere to go?'

'Every time I go out grocery shopping . . . somebody wants to pick the same avocadoes I'm looking at . . .'

'*Being able to socially distance is a sign of privilege.*'

UK arresting officer of homeless man: '*I am arresting him for breaching coronavirus conditions because he had no address.*'

'There are more important things than living and that's saving this country.'

N for Numbers

At the end of June 2020
confirmed Covid-19 cases
exceeded ten million globally.
As with war or famine or tyranny,
ten million
caught up involuntarily.

The good news is that deaths
were only half a million
but who is counting?

Numbers cannot convey
the mounting scale of loss.
Only those who feel it
– which is all the world –
know it.

Ye Housewife

Ye Housewife in her kitchen white,
She scours ye pots and pans;
She kneads ye bread, and bakes it too,
With ever busy hands.

B for Bread

The housebound
rediscovering

kneading dough as
the simplest of pleasures.

Making bread with
time on our hands

a substitute for the touch
we are so wanting

while fashioning
the staff of life.

J for Just

I just realized
the letter of the alphabet so far absent
from these Pandemic Poems
is the letter J
which is why there's not yet an ending.

Out there, every day
they keep calling the names
of the dead
Awaiting justification
Awaiting arrest
Awaiting judge and jury

Too much absence
of justice
for closure.

C for Chillin . . .

The demographic is changing. Now it is the young
contracting the virus as Covid-19 fatigue sets in.
When you are young, life is for living; the herd instinct
trumps dire warning.

We've all been there.

Social isolation is especially hard
when you have been cheated of Spring's promise.
You will seize Summer by default
before falling into
the dead of Winter.

H for Hope

Hope sat back, when Pandora
opened the box to unleash
every evil on mankind. Hope alone
stayed behind. Or so
the Greek myth said.
In no rush to scatter panic,
create pandemonium,
or pandemic, like the rest.

Hope is still there, inside the box,
waiting to be invited.

D for Disposable

It was not the end-of-July headlines
that frightened us: 'One death a minute
in the USA.' It is the way every day
the evidence piles up
to show how this virus is eating
the most vulnerable, how
the body politic in every country,
everywhere, is offering up
as sacrificial victims
the ones regarded as
throwaway citizens.

S for Sweep

All over the ruined city
the abrasive sound of broken glass
being swept up.

How many other cities are broken
and waiting to crack wide open?

How many broken lives
swept under the carpet?

Hold fast to this image
from the ruined city:
the beautiful bride
in her wedding dress
posing for the photographer
the moment the blast hit

And someone there to sweep her up
to safety.

C for Cruise

Cruise ships were the ultimate getaway, promising
the pleasures of escape. Until the pandemic
made them the incubators of bad news.

So why do I increasingly feel as if I've been
teleported to one? With a stern captain
reverting to celestial navigation,
with racketing, frazzled crew,
and us passengers,
masked and socially distanced,
hijacketed.

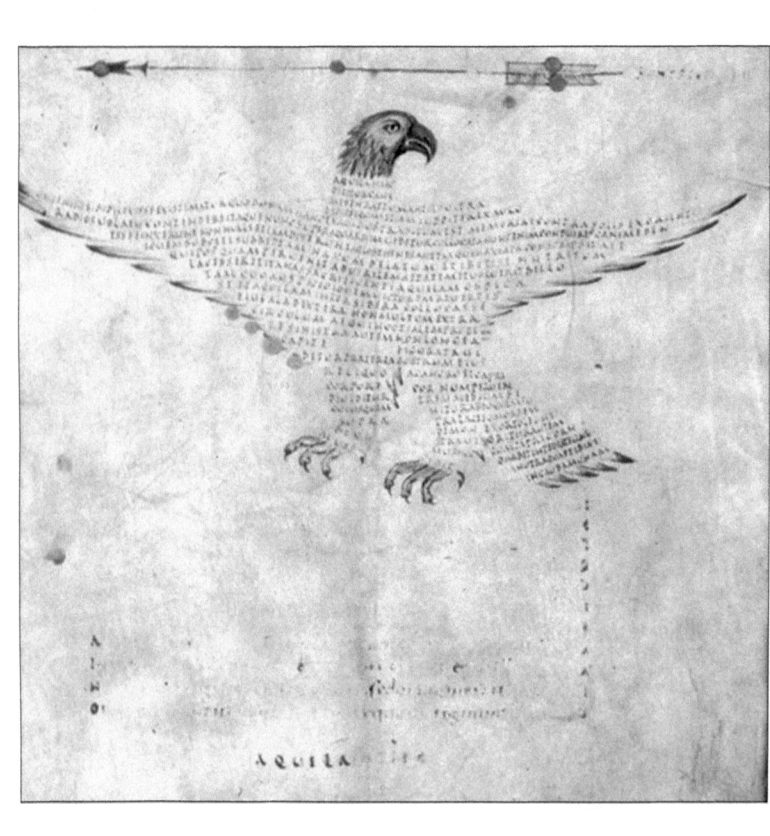

B for Bird 1–0 Technology

I know I shouldn't laugh because
this might be the precursor to
a more sinister scenario. But the headline
'Bald Eagle Attacks Government Drone'
is too good to dismiss. Attacked the drone
and dropped it with a *Hiss!*
into the depths of Lake Michigan.
What can this mean? I wish I had access
to an Augur whose duties included
ritual inaugurations and who could read
messages from the gods written in the skies.
Would this be read as foretelling
the triumph of light over darker forces?

But I suspect it is nothing more
than this: *Hiss!* Cross Nature showing us
once again who the bigger boss is.

W for Wrong-Sided

That Black Lives Matter T-shirt was probably sewn
by an exploited Black worker.

Most textile workers are women from the Global South.
They make $80–100 a month from garment assembly.

When the pandemic hit, US and European fashion brands
immediately cancelled or suspended orders.

Factories closed, workers were fired, lives unravelled.
In the global supply chain, garment workers are disposable.

Some factories are opening up again.
But, the fickle fashion industry needs a brand new model.

And you, fashion addicts (myself included),
you need to examine your consumption fetish

to make sure you won't be caught wearing a label
that puts you on the wrong side of an ethical verdict.

E for Empty

In the countryside, change moves to nature's rhythm.
In the city, it dances to jack hammer, crane,
and cement mixer.

Streetscapes shift overnight with knockdown. Holes
in the ground today, tomorrow a gleaming new tower.
So much so easily erased, so quickly replaced.

Would that some other empty spaces
could be so easily plastered over.

1007

Im m vii ior nach der gepurt Christi erschin ein wunderbarlicher
cometer, der gab feuer hin vund her, von im flamen, das er auff
die erden fiell, das geschen ist worden in deutsch welsch landt.

W for Warning

The Comet Neowise dropped in
from the outer regions
of the solar system. Described as
very photogenic,
it was the first comet visible to the naked eye
for a number of years,
leading to a photographic frenzy
to capture its flaming visiting card.

Comets are believed to foretell misfortune,
herald national disasters.

This comet's come and gone.
Doesn't plan to be back this way
for 6,800 years.
O dear.
Does that mean it signalled something
after all
that we failed to hear?

G for Gamble

The hazard now is how to balance
    risk versus necessity.
Do we dare or
Do we dare or
Do we dare to go out there
    and throw the dice
    play the game
Or do we sit at home alone playing
    Solitaire

B for Bees

I want to write an ode to bees, get down
on my knees (even though one recently stung me).

Not for the honey, or the wax, or the painful
sting, but because we owe them our continuing

existence. Bees fertilize while extracting nectar
and pollen to ensure the survival of their hives so

they are not working exclusively for us, but
their demise would also mean the end of our species.

One-third of the food we eat and most
flowering plants are fertilized by bees. Now they

are on their knees, their survival threatened by
habitat loss, toxic pesticides and disease.

Do your part: Respect trees. Plant flowers
to attract honeybees or bumblebees or any other.

The rose knows how to do it: scented handkerchief,
colour-coded message: *Buzz by, Honey, and kiss me.*

C for Circle

A linear world requires a certain kind of order
but humanity is programmed for the circular.

Communal gatherings, sports arenas, sewing bees
and teas, dinner time and story time – all facing in.

Perhaps for now linear is best since together
we are distanced and faceless.

One day soon, we will fall out of line, the bubble
will burst, the circle will enfold us once again.

Meantime, nothing is lost as long as every
individual heart is engaged in continuous circulation.

E for Ease

When the coronavirus pandemic began
those folks who monitor earthquakes
found high frequency noise reduced
in waves across the planet
as each country shut down.

I'd like to think (unscientifically) those diminishing
sound waves enabled grace notes not usually heard
above the din. Groans and sighs and moans and
whispers, burps and release of gases.

Mother Earth behaving exactly like an old woman
getting home after spending the day
with her rambunctious grandchildren,
taking off her go-to-town shoes,
easing out of her tight-fitting underclothes,
her Sunday best,
and in the welcome quiet, sitting at ease
in her rocking chair
thanking her Maker for (at last!)
a peaceful rest.

L for Less

There's no vaccine for Mother Earth.
The cure is more of a withdrawal:

Less
    toxicity
Less
    extraction
Less
    plundering
Less
    exploitation
Less
    consumption

A poisoned earth is squeezing us to death.

Ease up.
Nature is sending out an s.o.s

The only cure:
Less is more.

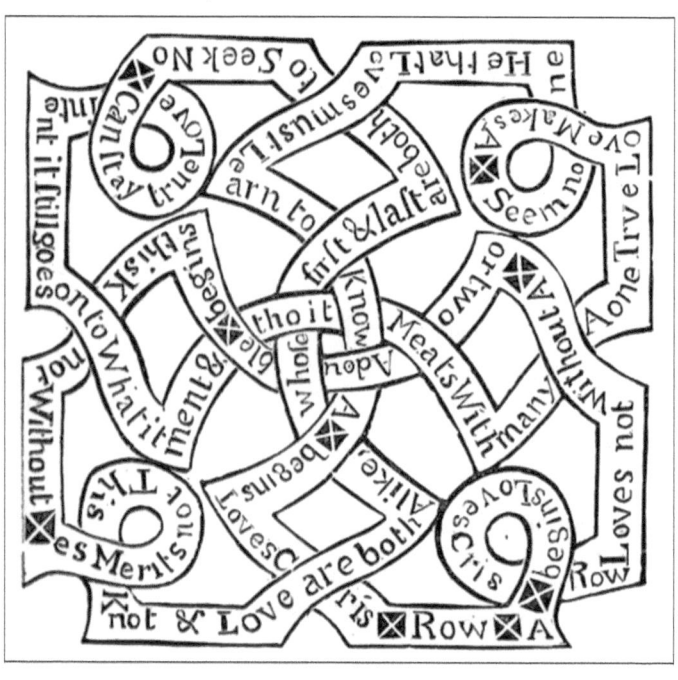

N for Negotiate

This word has come down in the world, the pandemic
shifting it from the formal sphere of business
to the social and domestic.

Everything in life has to be negotiated now.
Should I go?
Should I stay?
Should I send my child to school?
Virtual or real?
How should I meet and greet?

Not the recklessness of gambling with our lives but
the perplexity of making the right choices.

From our leaders, the only answers are non-negotiable:
    HANDS. FACE. SPACE.

There is no outside help for it.
Covid-19 forces individual bargains with the unseen.

Nevertheless, there's hope for you.
Negotiate also means
finding a way through.

L for Landfall

Birds are falling out of the sky
Nobody knows why.

Across the southwestern USA
masses of dead birds found.
Resident birds are safe and sound.
This toll is of migrants
on their annual round
long-distance flyers from the north
heading for their winter ground.

We don't yet know the causes
or the extent of the losses.

Just birds stressed
like the rest
of nature.

Ye Town Crier

L for Liberty

Government is taking liberties
with citizens, trying to mask them
and task them with sanitizing and
distancing when

> *We want to party*
> *We want to play*
> *We want to worship*
> *in our usual way*

The masks are off
the crowds are celebrating freedom
in Trafalgar Square and
everywhere

> Well, that's OK.
> Covid likes to see your face
> Covid likes a fight
> Covid is totally happy
> with parties every night

Let the rest of us not have to remember
September
as the month of
Give me Liberty and Give me Death.

ACKNOWLEDGEMENTS

Thanks to friends and family who encouraged me in the early stages and to fans on Facebook and Twitter. Your enthusiastic response to the Pandemic Poems postings kept me going.

To Shivaun Hearne and Sharmila Mohammed, who helped to make the book possible: "Good fren better than pocket money."

Illustrations

page 2: "A Vision of Isolating Technology", *Punch*, 26 December 1906, https://publicdomainreview.org/collection/a-vision-of-isolating-technology-from-1906

page 10: "Dr Alesha Sivartha, *Book of Life*" (1898), https://publicdomainreview.org/collection/diagrams-from-dr-alesha-sivartha-s-book-of-life-1898

pages 14, 52: "Lewis W. Leeds, *Lectures on Ventilation*" (1869), https://publicdomainreview.org/collection/illustrations-of-ventilation-1869

pages 26, 62: "A Nineteenth-Century Vision of the Year 2000", https://publicdomainreview.org/collection/a-19th-century-vision-of-the-year-2000

pages 39, 54: "Illustrated Initials from a German Fairytale Book (1919 edition)", https://publicdomainreview.org/collection/illustrated-initials-from-a-german-fairytale-book-1919-edition page 51: "Guess the Celeb Behind the Driving Garb (1906)", https://publicdomainreview.org/collection/guess-the-celeb-behind-the-driving-garb-1906

pages 56, 60, 86: "Woodcuts from 18th-Century Chapbooks", https://publicdomainreview.org/collection/woodcuts-from-18th-century-chapbooks

page 61: "Hamonshu: A Japanese Book of Wave and Ripple Designs (1903)", https://publicdomainreview.org/collection/hamonshu-a-japanese-book-of-wave-and-ripple-designs-1903

pages 66, 90: "Robert Seaver, *Ye Butcher, Ye Baker, Ye Candlestick-Maker* (1908)", https://publicdomainreview.org/collection/ye-butcher-ye-baker-ye-candlestick-maker-1908

page 69: "Olympic Diving Diagrams (1912)", https://publicdomainreview.org/collection/olympic-diving-diagrams-1912

page 74: "Aratea: Making Pictures with Words in the 9th Century", https://publicdomainreview.org/collection/aratea-making-pictures-with-words-in-the-9th-century

page 78: Augsburger Wunderzeichenbuch, folio 28, c. 1552, https://publicdomainreview.org/collection/flowers-of-the-sky

pages 80, 88: "*The World Turned Upside Down* (18th century)", https://publicdomainreview.org/collection/the-world-turned-upside-down-18th-century